Sticky Notes Volume 2

Trinette CollierGreene

Printed in the United States of America

Cover design by Elaina Lee
Page layout by FreedomInk Publishing
Initial edit by FreedomInk Publishing
Final proof by Trinette CollierGreene & Debra Palmer

First Printing, 2020

978-0-9861001-2-3

FreedomInk Publishing
P O Box 1093
Reidsville, Georgia 30453
www.facebook/FreedomInkPublishing/

Dedication

Sticky Notes... They Said What?!?! Classic Classroom Comedy Volume 2 is dedicated to ALL of the Extraordinary and DEDICATED Educators across the world. This is truly a hidden Blessing. Continue teaching from the heart and you will make a difference.

Special Dedication to My Parents, Ivory & Carolyn! I Miss & Love You Dearly! Thank You for sowing the seed... I Understand Now.

Cousin Daba
Fly High with Ivory Joe & Carol.

The FabFivePlus2
We Got This!

With Love, Mrs. CollierGreene
aka Ms. CollaGreene

Also by Trinette CollierGreene

Woman on Fire

'Sticky Notes, Volume 1... They Said What?!?!
Classic Classroom Comedy'

Sticky Notes
Volume 2

Trinette CollierGreene

First of All
First Grade Funnies

Him: "Ms. Collier, you look different today!"
Me: "Really?"
Him: "You look cute! You so beautiful!"
Me: Blushing.... "Awww, thank you sweetie pie!"
I gave him treats all day! :)

Career Choice

Her: "Ms. Collier, did you pay to be a teacher?"
Me: "Yes ma'am.... I paid a whole lot of money to be a teacher!"
Her: "I love teachers because y'all make us smart!"
Me: I just smiled as I thought of those student loans!

#FirstGrade

Me apologizing to a student:
"I'm sorry sweetie, I got to get your name right! That letter is confusing me. I promise I will learn it."
Her: "That's ok, you'll get it right! Just keep working on it!"

Coffee & Crayons

Him: "I smell coffee!"
Me: "Yepppp, mine!"
Him: "I love coffee!"
Me: Uhhhhh, you shouldn't be drinking coffee!"
Him: "I know… But I need it!"
Her: "Ms. Collier, do you need the lease to buy crayons?"
Me: "No, sweetie pie, I don't need your lease. We will supply you with some crayons :)

Tattletale

Him: "TEACHER!!"
Me: "Yes darling."
Him: "TEACHER!! He talking about God!"

☺

Best Crayon Ever

Students are coloring on white paper.
Him: "Oh boy! My white crayon is really working! I can't see it!"

Lights Out!

The power went out and of course the students need to use the bathroom.
One boy says: “Poor girls!”
Me: “Why did you say that?”
Him: “Poor girls ’cause they can’t see using the bathroom!”

Of course, the boys just aimed all over the place in the bathroom!
SMH

Spanish Gone Wrong

Girl: "Ms. Collier,
they talking nasty stuff!"
Me: "What are they saying?"
Her: "Stuff about butts!"
Boy: "No, I wasn't!
I was talking Spanish!"
Then he huffs and puffs, shakes his
head and says, "I don't know what I'm
saying because I'm talking Spanish!"
Me: "Well, what are you trying to say?"
Him: "I was talking about
my Momma in Spanish."
So I asked my bilingual
students to interpret.
Me: "Can you tell me what he said?"
They all looked at me like,
we don't know either!

Negotiations

Him: "Ms. Collier! I need another folder!"

Me: "Boy, I've supplied you with folders already."

Him: "Please Ms. Collier, I'll give you a bag of Cheetos!"

Me: "NO!"

Him: "Ms. Collier... Please?!?! I'll give you a juice! What about some candy? Huh?"

Me: "NO boy!! Now get back to work!"

Him: "OK, OK! What about some fruit? I KNOWWWW you like fruit!"

I just rolled my eyes and finished writing.

February

Her: "Harriet Tubman not dead, she went to sleep!"
#BlackHistoryMonth

☺

Hashtag #6

The light fixture falls out of place…
Him: "Oh Shit!"
Me: "BOY!!!!"

Person, Place or Thing

Me: "Someone give me a common noun."

Boy: "BOOTY!"

Me: "THAT'S IT! I'm writing you up!"

☺

Peace, Love and God

During a Dr. Martin Luther King, Jr. lesson…

Her: "I believe in God for peace and for us to love!"

Other girl: "Yeppp… You got to praise God, just be nice!"

It ain't Me!

Me: "Ewwww, who passed gas?!"
Several students yell out "Not me!"
Boy gets up and smells his seat and says, "Nahhh, that ain't me!"

☺

My Birthday!

Him: "Ms. Collier, the other day was
my birthday!"
Me: "What day was that?"
Him: "I don't know...
The OTHER day!"
Me: "Ok, I'll find that day for you!!" :)

Period

Him: "Girls wear diapers because they bleed all month!"
Me: "WHAT?!?!?"
Girl: "Boy! You don't know nothing 'bout that!"
Him: "I shol' don't!"

☺

Lost & Found

Custodian found a hat and asked the boys if it belonged to either one of them.
1st Boy: Takes a long sniff and states, "That don't smell like me!"
Custodian: "Ok cool!"

<u>Black History</u>

During Black History discussion...
Her: "Is there White History because we have Black History?"
Me: "Ohhhhh, yes baby! There is plenty of White History!"
#BlackHistoryMonth

Arts & Crafts

Her: "What's them things on your arm?"

Me: "Oh, these are bracelets that I made with my husband."

Her: 'What?? Yall bored or something?"

Me: "Nahhh girl, we try to have Arts & Crafts night!"

Her: "Oohhh yeah, that's a good idea!"

Me: "You can try it with your family!"

Her: "We shol' can! How I get them beads?"

Who Are You

First Girl: "'The Wiz' was African American?"
Me: "Yes… It is the African American version of the original movie, 'The Wizard of OZ'."
Second girl: "I wish I was African American!"
Third girl: "You IS!"
Second girl: "I am?! Ohhhhh!"

I think I need to incorporate MORE African American history!
SMH :)

Church Shoes

Our school Computer Technician walks in with black dress slacks, shirt and shiny black shoes. In the middle of my lesson, Boy yells out, "Mannnn, he got on church shoes! I like those! I got some church shoes like dat!"

Me: "Do you use them?"

Him: "Mannnnm yeah! At church! They my church shoes!"

His eyes stayed on the Tech's shoes the entire time he was repairing our computers!

Boys or Girls

Her: "How many children Dr. Martin have?"

Me: "He has 4."

Her: "What kind of children did he have?"

Me: "Huh?"

Her (stressing it even more): "WHAT KIND OF CHILDREN DO HE HAVE?"

Me: "What do you mean?"

Her (stressing it even more): "WHAT KIND OF CHILDREN DO HE HAVE?"

Me (unsure so I'm guessing): "Hmmm, boys and girls?"

Her: "2 boys or what?"

Me: "I'm sorry... Yes, 2 boys and 2 girls."

Her: "How he have 2 boys and 2 girls?"
Me: "Girlllll, ask your Momma!"

☺

Pre Planning

Her: "Ms. Collier, did you make plans for us last night while we were sleeping?"
Me: "Huh?"
Her: "You know? Instead of you sleeping, you supposed to be planning for today so we would know what to do for tutorial! And so you can know what to do for us."
I really couldn't say anything.....

End of The Day

Him: "Teacher! Somebody said Santa Clause ain't real! Tell him to stop saying that!"

Other Boy: "It's time to go!! YEYYYYY!"

Another Boy: "No it's not! School just started!"

It's 2:00 pm....

SMH

Using Resources

It's Spelling Test Day!
Me: "Boy! Stop cheating!"
Him: "I wasn't cheating! I was just looking at the words on the paper while we take the spelling test!"

☺

More Black History

Him: "White people are not African Americans! They can't be!"
#BlackHistoryMonth

Wardrobe Check

Her: "Ms. Collier! She pulling up my skirt!"
Me: "Heyyyyyyy! STOP THAT lil girl! Come here! Why are you pulling up her skirt?"
Other girl: "They said her panties are yellow and green and I wanna see! I gotta tell them no she ain't got yellow panties!"
Me: "GO TO YOUR SEAT AND DON'T MOVE!"

A Teacher's Truth

On this particular day, my little boy literally cried all day! He was adjusting to a new Step Mom and a new move.

Me: "Baby! Please stop crying! I can't handle it anymore because I don't know what to do.... I'm trying to help you but I don't know what to do.
Him: "I can't help it... I just don't know why I gotta come to school every day! Do I have to come Saturday too?"
Me: I looked at him and started crying too... "I know exactly how you feel bruh but it's something we gotta do!"
Him: (still sobbing but raised his head with some hope)

Me: “Can you please just work with me?”
Him: “I’ll try.”
Me: “Thanks so much…. I PROMISE I won’t keep you long!”

I am NOT making this up! LOL

The Brow

Him: "I wanna watch the Purge!"
Me: "NO! We are not watching the Purge and anyhow, that's inappropriate for you."
Him: "I don't care, I wanna watch it!"
Me, leaning back in my chair, thinking, 'Did he just raise his voice and tell me NO?'
Him, looking at me with THAT ready to challenge you look, and I'm looking back at him with that same look plus the Brow!
Me: "We AIN'T watching it!"

To The Moon

We were discussing the solar system and I asked if anyone had questions.

Him: "Ms. Collier, have you been to the moon?"

Me: "Nahhh, I haven't made it there yet!"

Her: "Awwww, you should go! It's fun!"

Me looking like 'Huh?'"

Another Girl: "My dad flies to the moon all the time!"

Other Girl: "I go to the moon all the time! It's fun!"

Him: "I went to the moon last night! It was cool!"

Other Boy: "My dad drives one of those!"

Me: "A Lunar Rover??"

Her: "Yepppp… He goes fast!"
Other Boy: "My dad is an astronaut!"
Me: "What's his name?"
Him: "Mr. C."
Me: "Oh ok!"

☺

I Was Born

As we cover the states on the map, the students are recognizing familiar states such as Florida, Texas, and Georgia and a random student starts to sing… "I was born by the river!"

Me, thinking, he must spend weekends with GrandMomma'em!

I'm Feeling Fine

Her: "You ok Ms. Collier?"
Me: "Yes, sweetie!"
Her: "Oh, cuz my Momma got some
pills for you if you need it!"
Me: "Ohhhhh.... No thanks sweetie...
I'm just fine!"

My Life Plan

Her: "Ms. Collier, is Chef Greene your boyfriend?"

Me: "Yes, he is," as I smiled.

Her: "Why didn't you tell us?"

Me: "I did introduce yall to him, remember? I told yall that he was my Fiancé and we were getting married."

Others: "Yeah but you didn't say to HIM!"

Me: "Huh? I did! He came to visit yall and I introduced him as my Fiancé, Mr. Chef Greene."

Him: "You gone get pregnant? You gotta get pregnant cause you will be married!"

Other Girl: "Yeah she is because she gotta have a baby!"

Other Girl: "It's ok to be married because you can't do it on your own!"
Other Girl: "You gone need a man because all that other stuff is hard work!"

I just placed my head on the table as they continued my Life Plan!

We Free

Watching an educational video on Harriet Tubman during Black History Month...

Her: "I'm gonna be free just like her!"
Him: "He know better to be talking to her like that!"
Another Boy: "Oh shoot! He touched her! We gotta do something!"
Her: "I'm never gonna be a slave!"

As I stepped out of the room for about 15 seconds...
Random students yelling out, "YEYY! We FREE!" "YESSS about time!" "She working us too hard!" "I'm tired just like Harriet Tubman!"

Private Parts

During our Social Emotional Learning (SEL) time, we are discussing the good and bad touch of our bodies including our private parts.

Me: "What are your private parts of the body?"

Various answers given by students included arms, eyes, nose, neck and so forth.

Boy looks around like, what in the heck are yall talking about?!?!

Him: "Those ain't private parts! My nuts are private parts!"

Girl: "Yeah and my vagina is private too!"

Other Boy: "And sometimes the boy puts his penis in a vagina, right Ms. Collier?"
Girl: "You have a vagina Ms. Collier?"
Me: "We are done with this lesson!"
Looking up and asking "WHY ME LORD?! WHY???"

When I Grow Up

Her: "I love you Ms. Collier!"
Me: "I love you back baby!"
Her: "Ms. Collier, what's your last name?"
Me: Looking at her... "Ms. Collier sweetie."
Her: "Oh, so when I grow up my name is gonna be Ms. Rogers?"
Me: "Yes ma'am sweetie."
Her: "I can't wait to grow up so my name can be Ms. Rogers like you!"
Me: "I can't wait either sweetie... You're gonna be so awesome!"

Girls Will Be Girls

Her: "Ms. Collier, you cute today!"

Me: "Thank you girl! So that means I can't fuss at yall today!"

Her: "Nope... You too cute!"

Me: "BAM!"

Her: "What's your first name?"

Me: "Trinette."

Her: "Really? Maybe it can be Collier Trinette"

Me: "Ooooh ok."

Her: "Can you do hair? I really need you to do my hair in a ponytail!"

Random Thought

Girl bursts out singing in the middle of my lesson, "Everybody hates Chrisssssss!"

☺

My Hair

We really should start school AFTER Labor Day!

Little Boy stopped at the door and yells out, "What happened to your hair?!"

Me: "I took out my braids. You don't like it?"

Him: "Nahhhh, my Momma can do hair! You want me to call her?"
Me: "Nahhhh, I have a *stylist*, I'm just letting it breathe."
He looked at me like.... Yeah ok!

☺

Texting While Teaching

While I'm actually giving Class Dojo Points from my phone, little girl yells out, "She texting her man yall!"

Bruh!

Him to another classmate,
"Bruh! You need to brush your teeth!
It's too early to have stank'n breffff!"

☺

T-T-Y

Some kids were singing a popular YouTube song… "P.E.T.T.Y, you petty… What? You petty!"
Him: "What the HELL is T-T-Y?"

Hashtag #6

Her: "Ms. Collier, do we have Girl Couts today?"

☺

The Blues

We were watching a grammar video on pronouns called 'The Pronoun Blues' and a student is making himself cry.
Me: "Why are you crying?"
Him: "I got the blues!"
Me: "Dang it! Let me cut this off!"

Teacher Moment

Them: "Good morning Ms. Collier."
Him: "Good morning Ms. Collier, I went to the crazy doctor yesterday!"
Me: "What?"
Him: "Yeah, I go to the crazy doctor because I can't sit down."
Me: "You ain't crazy baby... Now go sit down!"
He looked at me with a smile!
I smiled back :)

I REFUSE to speak THAT over their lives for a check!

Thomas

Teaching about Thomas Jefferson with pictures and a little girl yells out…
“He cute! I mean, he handsome!”
Me: “Glad you think so girl!”

☺

Hand Picked

Him: “Who’s gonna pick your husband?”
Me: “My husband is already picked.”
Him: “Ohhhhhhhhhhhhhhhh!“

Can I Get an Amen?

Me: "Class, what are your goals for next year in 2nd grade?"
Her: "To keep Praising the Lord because I know I'm gonna need Him!"
Me: "Yes girl!!!!!! YESSSSSS!"

☺

A Teacher's Truth

Viewing Harriet Tubman video and a little boy yells out, "This is for church!"

<u>Playa of The Year</u>

Him talking to another classmate...
"Boy, you aint' all that cuz you can't git no guls like me!"
Other Boy: "Yes I can! Watch me!"

He walked towards two girls with a book in his hand!

I just threw my hands up!

Four'Ever Shenanigans
Never A Dull Day In PreK

MidDay PreK Shenanigans

Her: "Mrs. Greene, I LIKE YOU!"
Me: "Awww! Thanks baby, I LOVE YOU TOO!"
Her: "No! I said I LIKE you!"
Me: "Oh, ok.... 😔"
She walks back to her cot smiling.
I'm sensitive today.

☺

Random Thought

Her: "Mommy is so serious!"

Dark White

Four-year-old is drawing Elsa's castle....

Me: "What's around the castle?"

Her: "Ice."

Me: "What color can you use to draw ice?"

Her: "Dark white!!!!!"

☺

Cut It

So.... As we are cutting on straight lines, a Pre-Kindergarten student begins to sing "The paper way too big we need to cut it!"

Testing Day in Pre-K

Me: "What sound do you hear when I say m-m-milk?"

Him: "CEREAL!"

Me: "What sound do you hear when I say s-s-six?"

Him: "SITDOWN!"

Me: "What sound do you hear when I say s-s-sick?"

Him: "When I was in da bed!"

Me: "What sound do you hear when I say m-m-meat?"

Him: "Chicken!"

Me: "What sound do you hear when I say b-b-bear?"

Him: "Eating somebody!"

Me: "What sound do you hear when I say s-s-sad?"

Him: "Just be Happy!"
Anddddddddd he was VERY CONFIDENT with answering like duhhhh!

19 more to complete!

☺

Storytime

The lady is reading a story and she is discussing nuts & berries...
A student yells out, "She nasty!! She likes nuts!!"

I turned my head and pretended I didn't hear.

Militant Brother

Him: "Why you got all 'dem white people on the wall? Y'all ain't got no black people!?"

Me: "Yes we do baby! We have many different people, look around the room!"

Him: Yeah but they over there, (pointing to the back of the room) and you need to put them right here (pointing to the front of the room) so I can see them!

Me: We do have two right there...

Him: "NOOOO! All of them right there! We black! They 'posed to be in the front! We ain't in the back!"

He wanted ALL of the Brown boys & girls in the front of the room... Not the back or side of the room.

Me: "Ok, I'll make the changes."

I am NOT making this up!

Another Teacher Truth Moment

Lil Lord Furquaad (his nickname) says to me: "Mannnnn why you always be mad?!"

Me: "'Cause you always yelling at me dude!"

Him: Shrugs his shoulders & walks out the classroom.

Me: Shrugs my shoulders and finishes completing certificates! 2 More Mondays.... 2 MORE MONDAYS!!

Brain Break

Him: "Teacher! My brain hurts! I don't wanna work."

Me: "I know baby. Your brain will hurt a lot more in kindergarten!"

He stared at me for a long time.

<u>Baa Baa</u>

Me: "Baa Baa Black sheep
Have you any wool?
Yes sir, yes sir
Three bags__________"
Him: "PLEASE!"
As he was supposed to complete the rhyme.

Bruh

Him: "Hey bruh! Hey bruh bruh!" (He was talking to me)
Me: "Hey baby, I'm not your bruh, I'm Mrs. Greene."
Him: "Hey Mrs. Greene bruh."
Me: "Boy?!! "

My Fro

Girl: "Ooowee... You need to do something about that Mrs. Greene!"
Me: "You don't like my fro?"
Her: "Nahhh, when you gone do something about it?"
Me: "I don't want to do 'something' about it!"
Her: "Yuppppp, you got to!"

A few days later, I walked in with cute braids and she was like.....

Her: "Oooooooooweeeeee Mrs. Greene, You did something about it! It's cute! Yuppppp! It's cute!"
I swear fo' gawdddd!
I gotta stay cute with this crew!

What Month Is It?

Me: "What month is it?"
PreK: "NOTEMBER!!"

☺

Coupon Diva

I didn't come to work yesterday so this morning, my girl rushed in with a great big smile and said:
Her: "Heyyyyyy Mrs. Greene! I got your Birthday gift!!" (Coupons)
Me: "Heyyy girl!!! I missed you!!"
Her: "Here's your gift! You can pick this," (pointing to the shakes and

burger). I have $2.00 so you can only get those."
Me: "No fries?!"
Her: "I guess you can, but I only have $2.00!"
Me: "OK.... I'll get the burger and smoothie."
Then she proceeded to sit at the table and go over the menu.... All she needed was a cup of coffee and reading glasses!
#Countdown
#IREALLYDOLOVEMYBABIES

Doggy Treats

Boy told his sister that I was feeding them dog treats! So she walked up to me with a very serious look and asked...

Her: "Mrs. Greene, why you feeding my brother dog food?!!"

Me: "HUH???? WHAT?!?!"

Her: "You feeding my brother dog food!"

Me: "No I'm not!" (Like, I sounded like a kid because I had an attitude now.)

Her: "Yes you are... What do you call these?!" As she handed me the bag.

Him: "Mrs. Greene, these my dog treats you gave us!"

Me: "No hunni... These are pretzels... I promise I ain't feeding y'all dog food!"

Her: “Ok...” But she side eyed me hard, as they strolled on off....

☺

#PreKTired

Boy runs in and yells “It’s the last day of school!!!!!!!!! Can we play?!”

Me: “NOOOOOOOO! It’s NOT THE LAST DAY!”

Other boy: “But I’m tired!”

Me: “Me too!!”

The entire room jumps up & down and has been on 100!!!!!

My Boo

Girl looks at my phone and sees my husband. She asks, "Who is that?"
Me: "My husband, Chef Greene."
Her: "Awwww, are you in love?"
Me: "Yes girl, that's my boo!"
Her eyes were beaming with joy!

HAPPY FRIDAYYYYY!

I was interviewed by the sibling of one of my PreK student, a SERIOUS first grader!

She walked around my room and asked the following;

What is it that I teach him?

Does he play all day?

Is he taking naps?

What are the plans for him this semester?

Afterwards, I directed her to our posted Daily Schedule and went over each activity. She said, "Oh ok, so y'all are really working in here!"

Me: "Yes, we try our best to make sure that learning takes place and I really thank you for our 'Preconference'!"
Her: "Ok, I feel much better... He is going to be good!"
Me: "I'm so glad I had this conference with you, can you sign this form?"
She stared at me like... 'Don't play!'

November Rules

A PreK girl gave me a candy bag that her Mom purchased...

She walks in the next morning and says, "Mrs. Greene, I'm gone need that bag back!"
Me: "Why? You gave it to me!"
Her: "Yeah, I know but my Mom was crazy and she didn't know what she was doing... It's really for me... So imma need it back."
Me: "Well, your Mom said I can have it!"
Her: "Nawww... She ain't thinking right... So imma really need it back!"
Me: "Nawww sista gullll... It's mine!"
I looked at her like 'WHETTTTT!'

She looked at me like.. 'Ohhhhhhhh so you have tantrums too?!'
Then she said: "You so crazy girl!"
Me: "Yelppppppppp!" 😝😝😝😝

It's my MONTH! How 'bout dat😝😝😝
#ILoveMyBabies #WeCoolLikeDat

☺

Militant Bruh

Him: "Mr. Greene. The tornado (really couldn't pronounce it clearly) was bad!"
Me: "Yes it was but I'm so glad you were safe!"

Him: "Jesus picked me up and I seen Him in the tornado!"
Me: "Who?!?!"
Him: "JESUS! I said! He was black and He had them other colors too! Purple, red, yellow..."
Me: "Ohhhhhh ok! All of the colors?!"
Him: "Yeah!! And His feet had hair!"
Me: "Oh Lawd!"
Him: "Yeah! I know!!"

I think this message was about the rainbow after the storm?!? I don't know but he was persistent in telling me! Lol!

#TeacherPower

Girl: "I like my sisters and brothers."

Me: "OK! Yeah, I like mine too! "

Girl: "I like boys! They so cute!"

Me: "Yeah, they are." 🤪😊

Girl: "I like girls."

Me: "OK! Cool."

Girl: "Mrs. Greene, what do you like? You like girls?"

Me: I'm looking at her and in my mind I'm trying to figure out how to answer this question without it leading to a CHAIN OF QUESTIONS... On this topic.

Her: "Mrs. Greene. You don't like girls Mrs. Greene?"

Me: "I Like M&Ms!"

They just stared at me andddddddddd just like that... New topic!!

A Day At the Aquarium

As we are enjoying the dolphin show at the aquarium, a very loud PreK boy in the midst of the crowd yells: "LOOK MRS. Greene!!! It's PEEEEEEE!! They PEE'n Mrs. Greene! YEYYYYYYYY!!! Looooook Mrs. Greene!!! You see!!!"
Another Boy: "YEAHHHH! That's peeeeeeeeeeeeee!"

The other boys all cheered and clapped as the dolphins put on their show and I just kept looking straight ahead because I knew if I had placed my hand over the leader's mouth, I would've become a hashtag!

THEN THE AQUARIUM HAD THE NERVE TO TURN THE WATER YELLLLLLLOWWWW!!!

☺

Hats & Wigs

Her: "My Grandma got lots of wigs and hats!!"

Teacher Tired

Teacher Tired is wayyyyyy different than just being tired! Just waking up from 3:30 pm because my day went like this.....

👩‍🏫 Listened to 15 (3 students were absent), 'What I got for Christmas' stories and you know the stories of 4/5 year olds are STRETCHED!!

👩‍🏫 Viewed 15 pairs of new shoes, outfits, pants & coats!

👩‍🏫 I had to take off a full SNOWSUIT with the jacket because he wanted to wear it!

👩‍🏫 6 new braided hairstyles with BEADS & ORNAMENTS! Not one FOCUSED girl!

👩‍🏫 Over half of the class just wanted to sleep.

👩‍🏫 Some wanted to walk out of the classroom to the bathroom & refrigerator like they were at home... So we had to REVIEW EXPECTATIONS!

👩‍🏫 A few asked me how come I didn't have my lashes on!

👩‍🏫 Some asked why my hair wasn't done, so they just looked at me like I could have done better! My appointment is Wednesday!

👩‍🏫 A few Mommas ain't got boyfriends no more! (Sipping tea)

👩‍🏫 And MORE!

THIS WAS ALL BEFORE 10:15 am

BUT I was glad to see that they returned to us safely❤

I done missed all kinds of appointments/phone calls/ etc… this afternoon!

☺

My Gift

Her: "I got you a gift Mrs. Greene!"
Me: "Awwww thank you!"
Her: "Here!"
Me: The kids usually tell me that I smell good (as I check myself).

Day 2 of No Coffee... It's gonna be a long day!

Morning Circle

I'm minding my own business as usual while the kids have their morning discussion. Somebody decides to let out a silent BUT STRONG GROWN-FOLK dose of human gas!

Boy #1 sitting next me yells out "Ewwwwwwwwwwwww Mrs. Greene! You FARTED!"
Me: "NO I DIDN'T!"
Him: "Yes you did! I smell you!"
Me: "NO I DID NOT! That wasn't me!"
Him: "I smell it... It's right here!"
Me: "Well, it wasn't me! It was one of your classmates!"
Now I have straight attitude because I'm going back & forth for about 5

minutes as it became intense because I know I didn't do it....
Boy #2 (The Farter) looked at me & I knew he did it so I looked at him and said, "Dude, really?! You really ain't gon' say nothing?!"

Him: "Nahhh...." as he smirked!

Me: "No snacks for you!"

Him: Yells out, "EXCUSE ME!!"

Me: With straight attitude... "Too late! How 'bout that!"

#Daba

Straight Juice... No Chaser

As I'm drinking my orange juice... (because I'm detoxing from coffee). Boy walks over to me and says... "Teacher! Is that liquor?"
I literally spit out my juice... Somebody bring a LARGE COFFEE!!!!!
I'm done DETOXIN!!

☺

They Are Listening

Him: "Teacher! My Momma got a man! But she don't like him!"

Me (I'm just listening)... "Oh ok... Well hopefully she will like him soon!"
Him: "Teacher, you got a man?"
Me: "Yes, he's my husband."
Him: "You like him?"
Me: "Yeahhh, I like him!"
Him: "Oh ok well my Momma don't like her man! She told him she don't like him..."
Me: "I understand baby... "It's like that sometimes."

Accountability Partner

As I was eating my local favorite breakfast from my favorite spot, minding my own business, my previous PreK student walked in and shouted...

"That ain't Strong4Life food Mrs. Greene!! You know better! You don't be listening to her (as she pointed to the intercom~Morning Announcements).

Then she started naming the foods I need! As she went down the list, I just kept eating.

This one is for you CuzzyDaba♥

Lil Deb Saves the Day

It was definitely a Friday Full Moon day!

Girl: "Teacher! I don't wanna learn nothing today!"

Boy: "Teacher! I NOT listening!"

Boy: "Teacher! My Momma outside... She told me to come (as he prepares to walk out!)."

Girls: Removing bows, barrettes all across the floor, shoes off, sharing gummies and snacks... BEFORE LUNCH TIME!

Boys: Wrestling, picking noses trying to see who has the biggest BOOGA! Like... They are sitting here digging and pulling out and showing each other!!

One digging in his butt 😳😳😳😳
Another one told me to smell his hands AFTER coming from the bathroom.
However, at the end of the day, during snack time, one of my babies said, "Here Teacher, I brought a snack for you!"
I was like, "Noooo baby, Momma got that for you!"
She then pulled out a second one out of a cute little lunch box and I was like AIGHT GIRLLLLLLLLLL!!! I cut it open in 2.2 seconds and sat there eating a Lil Debbie Snack Cake!!!
#LittleDebSnacksToTheRescue
#ILoveMyBabies

Thank You

My AWESOME, ACTIVE and
HILARIOUS Classes of 2018-2020

My FRamily
I LOVE YOU All!
Thank you for listening to my stories

My Mommy Greene
Thank you for encouraging me and
being GranMommy to my Babies

My Handsome Hunnie
Thank you for being a
TeacherHusband :)

My Management Team
The P.O.W.E.R Experience

Thanks for always thinking GLOBAL

My Publisher

FreedomInk Publishing

We going higher!

My Social Media Family

Thank you for being such a great audience and allowing me to SHARE and you LIKED :)

My STCLM Family

Thanks for praying and pushing

To My Scott Family

Thanks for being AWESOME EDUCATORS

Author Bio

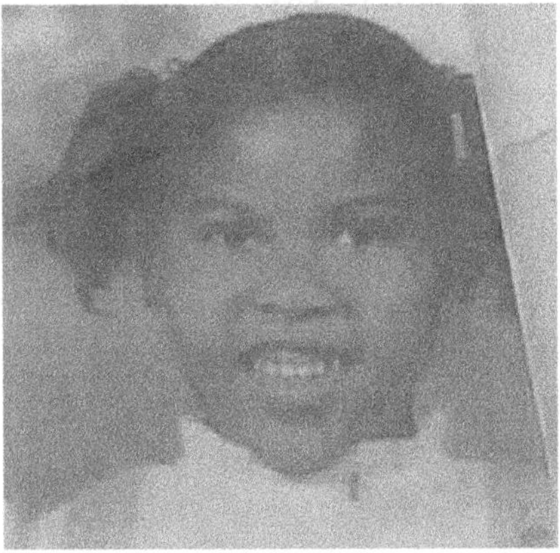

Trinette L. Collier Greene is a native of Los Angeles, California, who resides and teaches in Atlanta, Georgia. She is a nationally renowned Author, Certified Relationship Stylist, Educator, Entrepreneur and Radio Host. She is the eldest of the FabFive born to both the late Mr. & Mrs. Ivory & Carolyn Collier. Life as a military kid afforded her the opportunity to travel the world. It is through this that she gained life experience while living in different cities, states, and overseas. Her exposure to different cultures and ethnicities has led her to value and appreciate her very adventurous childhood. It is also through these experiences that she has been able to connect with the world at large, thus honoring her father's life's desire for his children.

Trinette received her B.S. in Early Childhood Education from Morris Brown College in Atlanta, Georgia and her M.Ed in Curriculum Instruction from Coppin State University. She is currently an educator with the Atlanta Public Schools system. Along with her formal career, she is also a Certified Relationship Stylist in which she owns and operates Trinette L. Collier, LLC.

In November 2013, Mrs. Collier Greene added to her notoriety and became a published author debuting her award-winning book, 'Woman On Fire'. In 2016, she added to her success the release of her second book entitled 'Sticky Notes, Volume 1... They Said What?!?! Classic Classroom Comedy'. Trinette currently resides in Smyrna, Georgia with her husband, Chef Greene. She is an active member of Strong Tower Christian Life Ministries and enjoys being with her family and friends. She loves music, dancing, helping others, learning, exploring new ideas, and more!

www.ingramcontent.com/pod-product-compliance
Lightning Source LLC
Chambersburg PA
CBHW062011040426
42447CB00010B/1997
* 9 7 8 0 9 8 6 1 0 0 1 2 3 *